YOUNG EINSTEIN IN
DISCOVERING SCIENCE

Welcome to our *Young Einstein* series of educational resource books, a series specifically designed to give young minds the tools they need to embrace and explore the mysteries and miracles of the world around them.

Each book is complete with clear text introducing the scientific principles, examples of those concepts at work, a step-by-step guide to explore each new concept, and further questions and ideas to urge young scientists on to more exploring.

The *Young Einstein* series is designed with any classroom in mind, aiding teachers and students both in the school environment and the at-home classroom by both educating children about the amazing world in which they live, and more importantly, giving young scientists the tools they need to explore and learn about their world on their own.

While having an adult's help is always important with the set-up and execution of experiments, each project in these books is specifically designed to place the ability to discover in the hands of young scientists. The pictures of each part of the experiments and interactive glossary are invaluable tools to aid young learners in their quest of understanding.

We are sure your young scientists will finish these books with a new understanding of the world around them, and newfound abilities to explore and discover their world on their own.

"Imagination is more important than knowledge. For knowledge is limited to all we now know and understand, while imagination embraces the entire world, and all there ever will be to know and understand." - *Albert Einstein*

© 2012 Flowerpot Press

Flowerpot Press
142 2nd Avenue North
Franklin, TN 37064

Flowerpot Press is a division of Kamalu, LLC,
Franklin, TN, U.S.A.,
and Mitso Media, Inc., Oakville, ON, Canada.

ISBN 978-1-77093-602-7

Illustrator: Tony Kenyon

Printed in China.

YOUNG EINSTEIN IN ACTION
DISCOVERING SCIENCE
Making Things Float & Sink

GARY GIBSON

FLOWERPOT PRESS
Nashville • Toronto

CONTENTS

INTRODUCTION

For thousands of years, people have built boats to sail on rivers and seas. Since then, we have been fascinated by things that float and sink. Why does a giant steel ship float, yet a single steel screw sinks? Why does ice float on water? How does a submarine both float *and* sink? How does a hovercraft travel on water *and* land? Why do some liquids float in water? This book contains a selection of exciting, hands-on projects to help answer some of these questions.

When this symbol appears, adult supervision is required.

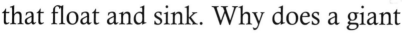

GET AN ADULT TO HELP YOU WITH THIS.

NOTE: Please use caution when doing each of the projects in this book. Some of these experiments can be dangerous. So, even when you don't see the symbol above, it is a good idea to have an adult nearby who can help you if you need some assistance.

WHY DO THINGS FLOAT?

Wood, cork, and ice all float, no matter what size or shape they are. However, materials such as oil-based modeling clay or steel sometimes float and sometimes sink. With these materials, it is their shape that decides whether they float or sink.

MAKE A MODELING CLAY BOAT

1 Fill a large plastic bowl with water.

2 Try to float a lump of modeling clay on the surface of the water. Try floating marbles, too. Watch them sink.

3 Using your thumbs, press the modeling clay into a boat shape. Hollow out the inside.

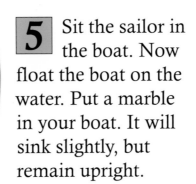

4 Draw a sailor on a sheet of cardstock. Color him in and cut him out. Fold along the dotted lines, as shown, so he can sit up.

Modeling clay sinks

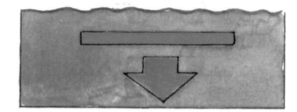

5 Sit the sailor in the boat. Now float the boat on the water. Put a marble in your boat. It will sink slightly, but remain upright.

Modeling clay and air float

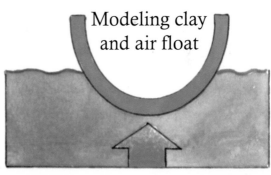

WHY IT WORKS

One teaspoon (5 milliliters) of water takes up more space than one teaspoon (5 milliliters) of modeling clay. Because modeling clay is denser than water, it sinks. Shaped into a boat, it fills with air. Air and modeling clay together are less dense than water, so the boat floats.

FURTHER IDEAS
Have a boat-building competition with some friends! Each person makes a boat using the same amount of modeling clay. Whose boat can hold the most marbles?

ICEBERG AHOY!

When most liquids freeze to solids, they become more dense. Water is different. When water freezes, it expands (causing pipes to burst in winter) and becomes less dense. Ice floats because it is less dense than water. Giant blocks of ice floating in the sea are called "icebergs." Ships have to be careful to avoid icebergs.

WATCH AN ICE CUBE BOAT MELT

1 Add enough food coloring to a jar of water to turn the water a bright color.

2 Pour the colored water into an ice cube tray, and put it in a freezer overnight.

3 Ask an adult to help you fill a large container with hot tap water.

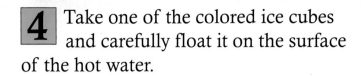

4 Take one of the colored ice cubes and carefully float it on the surface of the hot water.

5 As the ice becomes water, the color moves around in the warmer water. It sinks to the bottom of the container.

WHY IT WORKS

As the ice melts to water, its density increases. This makes it sink to the bottom of the container. There, it mixes with the water in the jar and warms up. It becomes less dense and moves back towards the surface.

Melted ice

FURTHER IDEAS Make a volcano! Fill a jar with hot water. Add food coloring. Cover the top of the jar with a paper towel held in place with a rubberband. Put the jar in a bowl of cold water. Pierce the paper. Watch the volcano erupt.

COLORFUL PAPER

It is not only boats and icebergs that float on water: oil-based liquids that are less dense than water also float on top of water. We sometimes see escaped crude oil floating on the sea in a thin layer that stretches for miles. Such oil slicks can harm the seabed, fish, and birds.

MAKE A COLORED PAPER

1 Ask an adult to mix a few drops of oil-based paint with a little bit of mineral spirits in a paper cup.

2 Place a bowl of water on some old newspapers. Add some paint and mix it into the water using a stick.

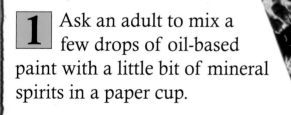

3 Carefully lower a sheet of plain paper onto the surface of the water. Let the paper soak up the paint.

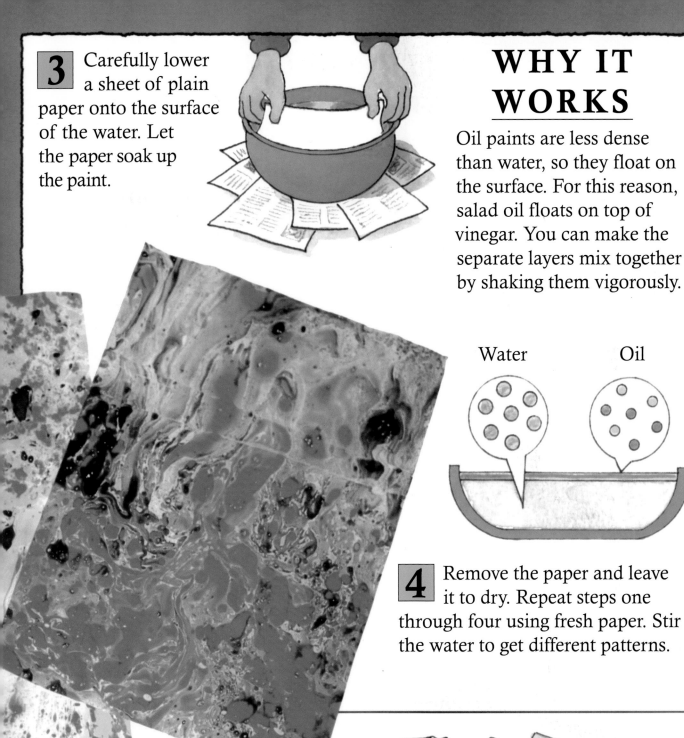

WHY IT WORKS

Oil paints are less dense than water, so they float on the surface. For this reason, salad oil floats on top of vinegar. You can make the separate layers mix together by shaking them vigorously.

Water   Oil

4 Remove the paper and leave it to dry. Repeat steps one through four using fresh paper. Stir the water to get different patterns.

FURTHER IDEAS
Try making different patterns by changing the colors of paint. Let the papers dry. Use your favorite patterns for stationery.

FLOATING LIQUIDS

Many liquids are similar to water and mix easily with water, but some liquids, such as oils and syrups, do not mix with water unless they are forced. Some liquids are less dense and float on top of water (see pages 10–11). Others are denser, so water floats on top of them.

MAKE LAYERS OF FLOATING LIQUID

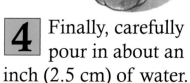

GET AN ADULT TO HELP YOU WITH THIS.

1 Find an empty plastic water bottle. Ask an adult to cut the top off with a sharp knife.

2 Slowly pour in some corn syrup so there is about an inch (2.5 cm) layer in the bottom. Let the corn syrup settle.

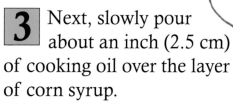

3 Next, slowly pour about an inch (2.5 cm) of cooking oil over the layer of corn syrup.

4 Finally, carefully pour in about an inch (2.5 cm) of water.

5 Examine the three layers. They float on top of each other without mixing. See what happens if you gently stir with a spoon.

WHY IT WORKS

The layers of liquid refuse to mix with each other. The corn syrup is at the bottom because it is the densest. The oil is the least dense of the three, so it floats on the very top.

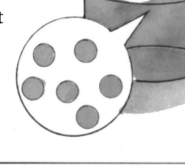

FURTHER IDEAS
Try floating different objects on your layers of liquid. Experiment with things that you would expect to sink in water.

FLOATING EGGS

How can you tell whether an egg is good or bad without breaking it? Fresh eggs sink if placed in a bowl of fresh water because they are denser than water. But if an egg turns bad, it floats in water. This is because the yolk and white have dried up, which makes it less dense than a good egg.

MAKE AN EGG FLOAT

GET AN ADULT TO HELP YOU WITH THIS.

1 Find two large containers. Fill one with hot tap water and the other with cold tap water. Get an adult to help.

2 Add a spoonful of table salt to the hot water. Stir in the salt until it dissolves completely.

3 Put a fresh egg into the salty water to see if it floats. If it doesn't, add more salt until it does.

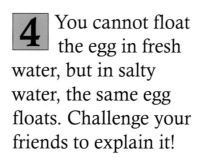

WHY IT WORKS

Salt dissolved in water increases the density of water. Denser liquids are better at keeping objects afloat. This is why many things that sink in fresh water will float in salted water.

4 You cannot float the egg in fresh water, but in salty water, the same egg floats. Challenge your friends to explain it!

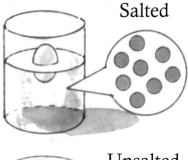

Salted

Unsalted

FURTHER IDEAS
See how long it takes for a fresh egg to go bad when not refrigerated. Test it in a bowl of fresh water each day. Dispose of the bad egg carefully when you've finished.

DIFFERENT DEPTHS

We have seen that each liquid has its own particular density. The denser, or heavier, the liquid, the better it is at making things float. Brewers of beer need to know the exact density of beer to ensure the beer tastes just right. A hydrometer is used to test its density.

MAKE HYDROMETERS

1 Pour equal amounts of syrup, cooking oil, and hot water into three containers of the same size.

2 Cut a plastic drinking straw into three equal lengths. Each will make a hydrometer.

3 Make three small balls out of modeling clay. Attach one to the end of each straw.

WHY IT WORKS

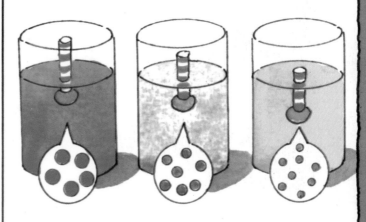

4 Carefully place one hydrometer into each liquid. Compare the different levels at which the hydrometers float.

The particles of dense liquids are bigger, or closer together. Dense liquids push harder on the hydrometer. The harder the push, the higher up in the liquid the hydrometer floats.

UNSINKABLE

Boats and ships are always built to be as stable as possible. This means that they do not get pushed over easily by waves in rough seas. Most boats and ships capsize and sink if they are pushed too far. A buoy is a channel marker. Because it is there to warn of danger, it is vital that it never gets pushed over.

MAKE A BUOY

1 Half fill a large container with water.

2 Find an old ping-pong ball. Paint it. Slice off the top of it. Make a hole in its center.

GET AN ADULT TO HELP YOU WITH THIS.

3 Fill the inside of the "buoy" with modeling clay and tape the top back on.

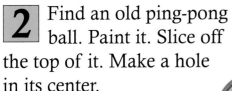

4 Make a flag out of a triangle of paper and a drinking straw.

5 Stick the flag into the hole in the top of the buoy.

6 Put the buoy in the water. Make some waves. See how difficult it is to push the buoy over.

The modeling clay acts as "ballast." A ballast is spare weight. The ballast pulls downward into the water and keeps the buoy upright. Boats carry a ballast to keep them stable at sea.

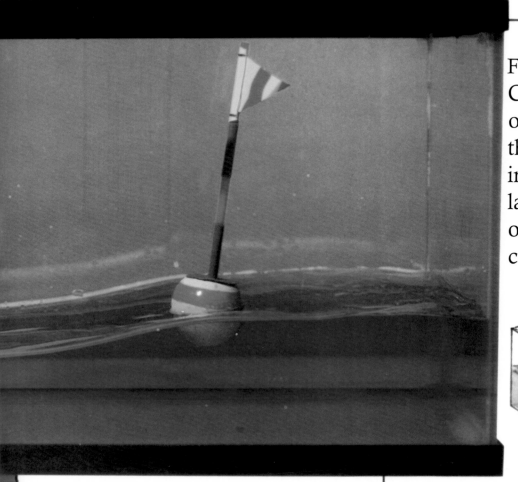

FURTHER IDEAS Compare the stability of your buoy with the boat you made in Project 1. Waves lapping over the side of the boat can easily cause it to capsize.

PORT AND STARBOARD

At sea, sailors say "port" for left and "starboard" for right. Ships and large boats have steering wheels, while smaller boats have a tiller instead. Both wheel and tiller are used to control a "rudder." The rudder is used to steer the boat.

MAKE A BOAT WITH A RUDDER

GET AN ADULT TO HELP YOU WITH THIS.

1 Ask an adult to cut a boat shape from a piece of polystyrene plastic. Make two holes as shown.

2 Make a brightly colored sail out of thin paper. Push a wooden stick through the sail.

3 Push the stick into the hole at the pointed end of the boat. Hold in place with modeling clay.

4 Cut a rudder out of a waterproof drink carton. Tape it to a drinking straw.

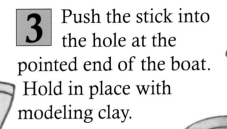

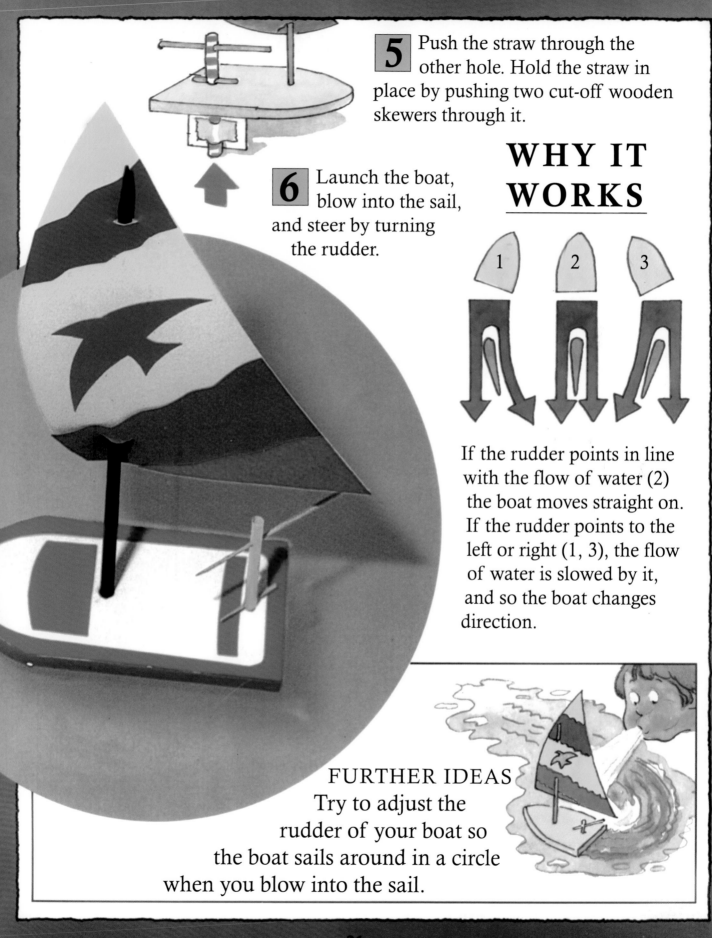

5 Push the straw through the other hole. Hold the straw in place by pushing two cut-off wooden skewers through it.

6 Launch the boat, blow into the sail, and steer by turning the rudder.

WHY IT WORKS

1   2   3

If the rudder points in line with the flow of water (2) the boat moves straight on. If the rudder points to the left or right (1, 3), the flow of water is slowed by it, and so the boat changes direction.

FURTHER IDEAS
Try to adjust the rudder of your boat so the boat sails around in a circle when you blow into the sail.

JET POWER

Most boats and ships have propellers, which push them along. The propeller cuts through the water, pushing it back behind the vessel. This push against the water "propels," or makes the vessel move forwards. A jet-propelled boat can travel at high speeds without a propeller. The "jet," or fast-moving flow of water, pushes the boat along.

MAKE A JET BOAT

1 Decorate an old plastic water bottle. Weight the bottom of the bottle with modeling clay.

2 Ask an adult to make a hole near the bottom of the bottle.

3 Place a balloon inside the bottle. Make sure you do not drop the balloon.

4 Stretch the balloon neck over the sink. Fill the balloon half-full with water.

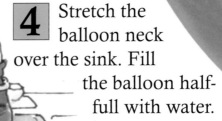

5 Pinch the balloon neck closed. Put modeling clay around the bottleneck to weight the bottle.

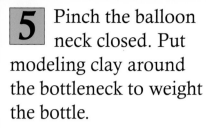

6 Still holding the end of the balloon, put the bottle in the bath.

7 Let go of the balloon. Watch the jet of water shoot out and push the boat along.

WHY IT WORKS

Boat moves forwards

Water out

When the water shoots out of the balloon, it pushes against the water in the bath. This pushing force propels the jet boat forwards. The quicker the water escapes from the balloon, the faster the boat travels.

FURTHER IDEAS

Cut a boat shape out of cardstock. Make a hole near the stern (back) of the boat. Cut from the stern of the boat to the hole. Float the boat. Drop dish soap in the hole. The boat will shoot forwards.

DIVE DEEP!

Deep under the oceans are some of the last unexplored places on Earth. Deep-sea divers use vessels that can sink to the bottom of the ocean and then float back to the surface again. Some marine animals, such as jellyfish, are also able to dive to great depths, then surface again.

MAKE A DIVING JELLYFISH

1 Find a large, clean plastic water bottle. Fill it up to the top with tap water.

2 Cut both ends off a flexible plastic drinking straw to make a "U" shape.

3 Unbend a paperclip. Bend it into shape shown at right. Push it into the ends of the straw.

4 Roll out three thin strips of modeling clay. Loop them around the paperclip.

WHY IT WORKS

When you squeeze the bottle, water is pushed into the straw, compressing the air. Water weighs more than air, so the jellyfish gets heavier and heavier.

5 This is your jellyfish. Drop it into the bottle and screw the top back on. To make the jellyfish dive, squeeze the bottle.

FURTHER IDEAS
Try making a diver from a small eye-dropper. Fill the dropper almost to the top with water, then put it into the bottle of water.

FLOATING UNDERWATER

Submarines are special floating vessels because they can sink and then return to the surface. Ballast tanks control how deeply they dive. To make the submarine sink, the tanks are filled with water. To make the submarine rise, the water is pumped out and replaced with air.

FLOATING UNDERWATER

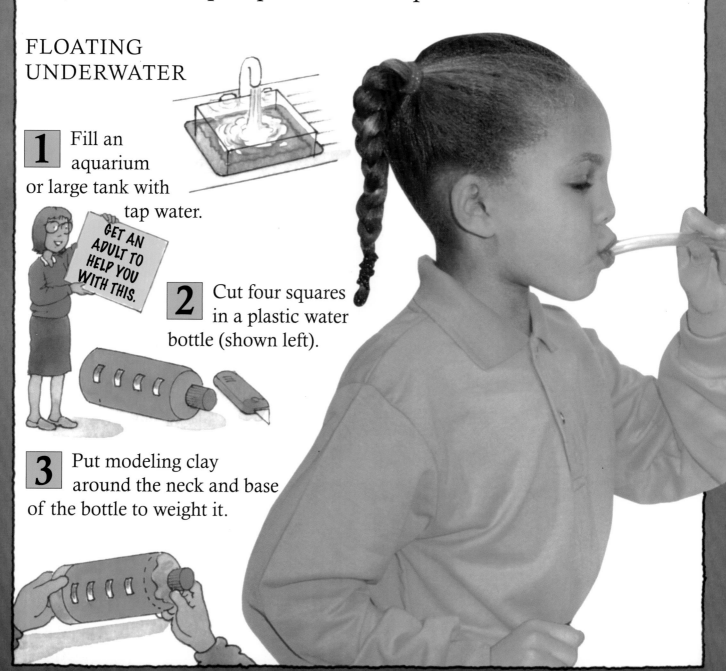

1 Fill an aquarium or large tank with tap water.

GET AN ADULT TO HELP YOU WITH THIS.

2 Cut four squares in a plastic water bottle (shown left).

3 Put modeling clay around the neck and base of the bottle to weight it.

4 On the other side of the bottle, make three holes, one large enough to fit a plastic tube.

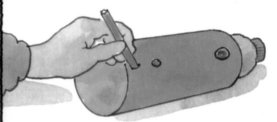

5 Decorate your submarine. Push the end of the tube into the larger of the three holes.

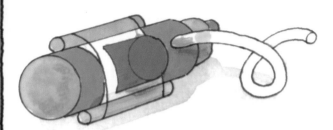

6 Try out your submarine. It will fill with water and sink. Blow into the tube to make it rise.

WHY IT WORKS

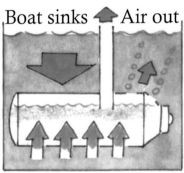

Boat sinks — Air out

The submarine sinks when it fills with water. When you blow into the tube, the water is forced out and replaced by the air. Air is less dense than water, so the submarine surfaces.

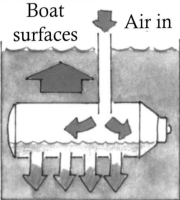

Boat surfaces — Air in

FURTHER IDEAS Put an empty bottle in the bottom of your aquarium. Let it fill with water. Now blow air into it with a straw to make the bottle rise.

FLOATING ON AIR

The hovercraft is one of the great inventions of the twentieth century. It can travel on water or on land. The engines suck in air and then pump it downwards. This creates a cushion of air that keeps the hovercraft from touching the surface over which it is traveling. The passengers enjoy a smooth, bump-free journey.

GET AN ADULT TO HELP YOU WITH THIS.

MAKE A HOVERCRAFT

1 Ask an adult to cut the top off a plastic water bottle.

2 Wrap some modeling clay around the base of the cut-off bottle top.

3 Make a skirt of paper to go around the modeling clay. Make sure it hangs over.

4 Blow up a balloon. Pinch the end. Carefully wrap the balloon around the bottleneck without letting it deflate.

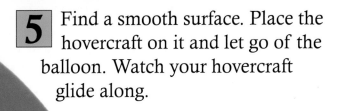

5 Find a smooth surface. Place the hovercraft on it and let go of the balloon. Watch your hovercraft glide along.

WHY IT WORKS

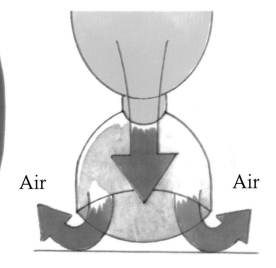

Air   Air

Air from the balloon escapes into the bottle top. The air pressure builds up until it creates a cushion that lifts the bottle slightly. It is the downward force of air that makes the hovercraft hover.

FURTHER IDEAS

Cut a hole in the bottom of a plastic margarine tub. Turn it upside down and fill it with air from a hairdryer. Watch it hover. Fill a paper bag with hot air from a hairdryer. What happens?

FANTASTIC FLOATING FACTS

Did you know that Aborigines are thought to have crossed from New Guinea to Australia in double canoes as long ago as 55,000 BC?

The *Titanic*, built in 1912, was claimed to be the unsinkable ocean liner. Tragically, on her first voyage across the Atlantic, she hit an iceberg and sank. More than 1,500 of the 2,200 people on board lost their lives.

The marine jet engine was invented by a New Zealand engineer named Sir William Hamilton in 1955. He tested his first jet boat in the shallow, fast-flowing rivers of New Zealand's South Island and it was one of his boats that was the first to travel through the Grand Canyon.

The first ocean liner ever to be made out of iron and driven by a propeller was the *Great Britain*. Designed by engineering genius Isambard Kingdom Brunel, the *Great Britain* embarked on her first voyage in 1845.

The deepest dive by a submarine was made by the United States Navy's deep submergence vessel, *Sea Cliff*, in March, 1985. It reached the incredible depth of 19,685 feet (6,000 meters).

The largest aircraft carriers in the world belong to the U.S. Navy. The *U.S.S. Nimitz* weighs more than 90,000 tons, is 1,059 feet (323 meters) long, and can carry 90 aircraft and a crew of about 5,700.

Plimsoll lines are marks on the side of a ship that indicate how much cargo can safely be loaded. Plimsoll lines show how low a vessel is lying in the water. The name comes from Samuel Plimsoll, who, in the nineteenth century, fought for safer working conditions for merchant sailors.

The first-ever submarine was built in 1620 by a Dutchman named Cornelius Drebbel. It was made out of wood and was propelled by using oars.

GLOSSARY

Ballast
Extra weight carried by vessels. It can be solid or liquid. A ballast helps keep a boat stable. When pumped out, it helps increase buoyancy.

Buoyancy
The ability of a substance to float. Buoyancy depends on the density of the object.

Compress
Squeeze together into less space.

Density
The weight, or heaviness, of an object when it takes up a given amount of space.

Force
A push or a pull that makes an object change direction.

Hydrometer
Instrument used to measure the density of liquid by how deeply it sinks into the liquid.

Jet
A fast-moving flow of water or air forced through a small outlet.

Port
The left side of a boat or ship, when standing on the boat, facing forwards.

Pressure
The force which presses down on a given area.

Propeller
A rotating object with spiral arms used to drive a boat or other vessel forwards.

Rudder
A flat steering object found under the stern (back) of and underneath a boat.

Stable
Steady; not easy to push over.

Starboard
The right side of a boat or ship, when standing on the boat, facing forwards.

Tiller
The handle used to turn a rudder.

Volume
The amount of space something takes up.

INDEX